# To Make an ISLAND
## OF A STREET CORNER

### BY ANACAONA ROCIO MILAGRO

Copyright © 2024 Anacaona Rocio Milagro

First Edition, 1st Printing

ISBN 13: 978-1-955953-04-7

Editors: Jehan Roberson, Ishion Hutchinson, Caroline Rothstein, Lisandra Ramos, and Tali Gumbiner

Cover / Interior Design: Rico Frederick / DizzyEngine (ricofdk.com)

Black Freighter Press
San Francisco, California

https://www.blackfreighterpress.com/

# Table of Contents

1. *Dedication* .................................................................................................. 1

## I. Shipwrecked

2. Water Fear ............................................................................................. 4
3. Lunch Lady Jackie .................................................................................. 5
4. Shipwreck Poem .................................................................................... 6
5. Almost .................................................................................................. 7
6. Narratives: Three Lies & A Truth ........................................................... 8
7. The Night i Watched my 12 yr Old brother Get Cuffed & Taken From Our home, Tearing, Saying: "i didn't do it!" (Part 1) ........................................... 11
8. A Sonnet for The Monster Mr. Lee ....................................................... 12
9. The Night i Watched my 12 yr Old brother Get Cuffed & Taken From Our home, Tearing, Saying: "i didn't do it!" (Part 2) ........................................... 13
10. Lost Seed: An Abecedarian for Fatherless Daughters ............................ 14
11. The Night i Watched my 12 yr Old brother Get Cuffed & Taken From Our home, Tearing, Saying: "i didn't do it!" (Part 3) ........................................... 15
12. Without Grammar ................................................................................ 16
13. The Night i Watched my 12 yr Old brother Get Cuffed & Taken From Our home, Tearing, Saying: "i didn't do it!" (Part 4) ........................................... 17
14. She Looks Like Nirvana ........................................................................ 18
15. What a Pretty Little Girl ....................................................................... 19
16. As You Slept ........................................................................................ 20
17. The Real Miracle .................................................................................. 21
18. To Deify a Roach: An American Horror Story ....................................... 22

## II. Delirium

19. Disguise as a Self Portrait ............................................................26
20. 100 Centre Street: Criminal Court ...............................................27
21. Survivor's Guilt: A Villanelle .......................................................28
22. Love Like New York City Trees ..................................................29
23. Pep Talks: A Hood Girl Goes to College .....................................30
24. Sangana: A Good Girl Disease .....................................................32
25. Pep Talks: A Hood Girl Dodging Assimilation ............................34
26. Nine Eleven Poem .........................................................................35
27. Nine Twelve Poem ........................................................................36
28. When You Were Red .....................................................................38
29. *Stillmatic* ....................................................................................39
30. Delirium ........................................................................................40
31. How to Break Your Mothers Heart ...............................................42
32. Blue Passport .................................................................................43
33. La Boca de Nigua ..........................................................................44
34. |Absolute Value| ............................................................................45
35. Pep Talks: A Hood Girl in Corporate America .............................47
36. Rose was a rose was a rose ...........................................................50
37. Emissaries and God Bodies ..........................................................51

## III. Fear of Water

38. *The Raft of the Medusa* .................................................................... 53
39. Dead President$ ............................................................................ 54
40. Water Fear .................................................................................... 55
41. Ge-he-na ...................................................................................... 56
42. *Born in Babylon Both Nonwhite & Woman* ....................................... 57
43. Percussion ................................................................................... 60
44. Nirvana Sky .................................................................................. 61
45. Stormborn .................................................................................... 62
46. Eat Their Young ............................................................................ 63
47. For The Days I Don't Love NY Because I Missed My Train, Was Already Late, & Then Gave My Orange Juice Away ................................. 64
48. Dear Lover ................................................................................... 65
49. *Gold Griot* .................................................................................. 66
50. Desahogarse: Undrowning (Suéltame Sataná) ................................. 67
51. Fear of Water ............................................................................... 69

**Notes** ............................................................................................ 72
**Acknowledgements** ..................................................................... 73
**Thank Yous** ................................................................................. 74
**Author's Bio** ................................................................................ 75

*Dedicated to*

*my beloved mother
and brothers*

*my children
Nirvana Sky and Zion*

*All safety is an illusion.*

—*James Baldwin*

# Shipwrecked

# Water Fear

The tides do not pause and wait
for you to catch your breath
Expect no kindness here

# Lunch Lady Jackie

She was bad. A cool bad.
All third graders wanted bad like hers.
i'd wait on line just to say *Hi lunch lady Jackie!*

Her sass: a dash of iodized smiles
like salt and hash to my bland-ass ham sandwich.
Tall, strong, witty. Epic ebony.

Tupac's tattooed Nefertiti
immortally pretty, lunchroom celebrity
my favorite lunch lady Jackie.

She was bad two years later when i saw
she made an island of a street corner.
Face frozen, blind to me watching her

twitching and begging, addiction napalmed
my ten-year-old eyes. The cafeteria window
faced the school's giant 'Crack-is-Wack' sign—

a mural on a twenty-foot concrete slab like
a tombstone where we played handball in the
playground outside the lunchroom.

At nightfall fiends morphed, made a restaurant
of our handball court. Syringes like forks
they dined until they starved, left empty

vials in our park.
i once waited outside

just to say *hi.*

# Shipwreck Poem

    Do not look for a ship    in this poem    you will not find one—
just the wreck.

   There is no mention of tumultuous sea journeys    or Tempests    or Odysseus
or whales   or       the stomach of whales.

What torments the night    to make it dive and rip sails    will not be unveiled
    —just the wreck.

   Because this is a shipwreck poem    you will find    the ship destroyed.
Pieces repurposed—    bassinets made of driftwood,    blood & salvaged hope.    You will be enveloped  by the   stench   of seaweed and vomit.    You will find a
    people   stuck.                 Isolated.
In an environment not suited for long life.    You will fall asleep hungry.    Awaken hungry.
Spend the day   with your   stomach   pulling the rope  of your tongue. You will be   chased.
   You will   run for your life   up crumbling mountains   down filthy stairwells   live in
    crumbling housing   panic often   have night terrors    in broad daylight.

   Because so much of a shipwreck poem is to do with delirium—a common symptom of being castaway.   You will find sanity   in suicide.  Merciful. You will   keep the dead as friends.  Religion   will be caught between    fable, faith and rage.  You will   hear screaming & crying.  Every so often   you will find    a floating body face down in the river and you'll
   keep drinking.   You will build a raft of music wax melded   broken beats   mended
   needle &   threaded into beautiful collages— the world will listen in  devotion
but ignore your cry for help.

   Let me tell you   how   little   is written   by   born castaways

Because this is   my   shipwreck poem   a 1980's baby up the street of New York City where
  i grew up   you'd find   a hollow library   where my overdue mother   resorted   to fish-out books from the garbage  to nourish  a young poet; an avenue   that harbored   the source outbreak  of the war-on-drugs crack epidemic. Scattered puddles of  green glass bottles—
    emptiness   the note.   You will find   people substitute   anything   for a boat.

For those of us born of this   wreckage   you will find our muscles  sore—   spasms   from unremembered storms.   You will find   our arms like broken oars   make   escape hard.
   How we try   only to redesign   the same disaster   because the wreck   is all we know.

   Because this is   a shipwreck poem   —most important of all—   you will face   an

ocean             that swallows and hoards   all   that is meant for you.

# Almost
*Dedicated to D. Martinez & Julia P.*

She isn't tired from swimming through dark rivers
or propelling her four children in tires
through the border—said she kept it simple
even played games, stopped the kids from crying.

She isn't tired, she swallows fears and sorrows.
Country on fire, she can't reconcile home.
Aborted her atlas of tomorrows
left behind all she's ever known and owned.

She isn't drained from learning a new language
or from dodging the drills of ICE EROs—
"Don't *aliens* come from other *planets*?"
daughter asking what makes them a third world.

Trying now with no rivers, roads, license—
it's the belonging that gets exhausting.

# Narratives: Three Lies & a Truth
*after Terrance Hayes, The Golden Shovel - dedicated to Nathan Englander*

I heard all white people crawled out of caves with tails from the cold North. Someone said, "If God wanted the white race to survive, their skin would drink the sun." Someone yelled "You're going extinct! Mixing with other races to survive. Nice try neanderthals. But you're still going to die off like the white moths cause you're nature's failed experiment." I heard whites love to have sex with their siblings, have cycloptic children hidden in basements, and never ever tell anyone about them. I heard whites aren't even Homo Sapiens, genetically not-human, another lesser species that lacks empathy, craves power, sociopaths that get off on another person's suffering. Devils are white, true colors burn red when exposed to natural light. I heard a story

someone said all Black people came from monkeys and never evolved. Genetically known to be more like apes than humans. Crazed to rape white women. Dangerous violent savages. Sure to steal. Super predators needing to be disciplined or they'll kill themselves. Dirty, lazy, you can't trust them—they're Godless, disease-ridden, ugly & unruly. Someone said, "they never get anything for themselves, always want handouts. They'd be dead or still swinging off trees if it weren't for colonization. Extra thigh muscle but of lesser intelligence—unaware of what's right"

I heard Race Horses want to be killed when they can no longer run. I heard their masters get to put them out of their misery. Thoroughbreds live to run & run to live & when they get hurt, it is truly the end of their world. Healing is not an option. They want to die and death is their right.

# Narratives: Three Lies & a Truth (continued...)
*after Terrance Hayes, The Golden Shovel*

I heard some demons crawled out of caves with tails from the cold North. Angels said, "If God wanted demons to thrive, their skin would drink the sun." Some angels yell "You're going extinct! Demons mixing with humans to survive. Nice try Lucifer. You're all still going to die off like the white moths cause you're God's failed experiment." I heard demons love to have sex with humans, have translucent children dominating media messaging, and tell all to follow them. Demons aren't Homo Sapiens but can genetically test human, create another lesser species that lacks empathy, craves power, sociopaths that get off on another person's suffering. Demons lack flight, true colors burn red when exposed to natural light. I heard a story

someone said white people came from monkeys and never evolved. Genetically known to be more like apes than humans. Crazed to rape all women. Dangerous violent savages. Sure to steal. Super predators needing discipline or they'll kill everyone else. Dirty and lazy, you can't trust them—they're Godless, disease-ridden, ugly & unruly. Someone said, "they never get anything for themselves, just take whatever they want. They wouldn't know how to bathe if it weren't for colonization. Extra germs and of lesser intelligence—unaware of what's right."

I heard Black people want to be killed when they can no longer work. I heard their masters get to put them out of their misery. Thoroughbreds work to live, live to work, when they get hurt, it is truly the end of their world. Healing is not an option. They want to die and death is their right.

# Narratives: Three Lies & a Truth (continued...)
*after Terrance Hayes, The Golden Shovel*

I heard women crawled out of caves with tails from the cold North. Some man said, "If God wanted women to thrive, he wouldn't have resurrected a son." Some man yelled, "You're liars & leeches! Sleeping with anyone to survive. Nice try you whores. But you're still going to die off like the white moths because you're God's failed experiment." I heard women love to have sex for riches, are heartless bitches, strategically have children to trap men, and forever tell tales as victims. I heard women aren't even Homo Sapiens but genetically test human, another lesser species that lacks empathy, craves power; sociopaths that get off on another person's suffering. Women are devils. Bleed red for six nights, breed sin in natural light. I heard a story

someone said Man came from monkeys and never evolved. Genetically known to be more like apes but less civilized, inhuman. They rape & pillage. Dangerous violent savages. Sure to steal. War hungry predators needing discipline or they'll kill themselves. Dirty, lazy, you can't trust them—they're Godless, disease-ridden, ugly & unruly. Someone said, "they never get to enlightenment cause they take whatever they want. They'll be dead before killing the trees; it is the guns, germs, and stone hearts. All muscle, low intelligence, unaware of what's right."

**3.**

I heard Gods want to be killed when they can no longer serve. I heard their masters get to put them out of their misery. Gods serve to live, live to serve, & when they don't serve, it is truly the end of the world. Healing is not an option. We will die and death is our right.

# The Night i Watched my Twelve-Year-Old Brother Get Cuffed & Taken from our Home, Tearing Up, Saying: "i Didn't Do It!"
## (Part 1)

birds living in a quiet corner of earth
must have burst open
mid-flight
staining the glass of sunset

without witness

# A Sonnet for The Monster Mr. Lee

> **For Mr. Lee:** *You are nothing like my father.*
> *And like my father*
> *you are nothing.*
> *—Eduardo C. Corral*

Her eyes replaced by teeth—sharp as can be.
Pulling her lips tight when we misbehaved,
irate, Mom threatened to wake Mr. Lee.
At home, our bodies brailled love's raged conceit.

Mom woke him, as he spoke our thighs would welt.
Lesson transcribed, whipped good under our clothes.
Lash after lash/ blow on blows/ scribe skin swelled.
Pleading was futile/ often made things worse.

Mr. Lee licked old leather and cold steel,
man of the house—the code-name for her belt.
Ten slashes/ ten syllables/ brace/ jump/ squeal.
We're better because of it/ her heart felt:

> *I/ don't/ want/ to/ have/ to/ do/ this/ to/ you./*
> *You/ know/ I/ do/ this/ be/cause/ I/ love/ you./*

## The Night i Watched my Twelve-Year-Old Brother Get Cuffed & Taken from our Home, Tearing Up, Saying: "i Didn't Do It!"
### (Part 2)

i was ten
his right hand, his confidant.

he was my
favorite. my
playmate, my
best friend
of my three older brothers—
playing wrestling, he'd tag me in
so his baby sister could play too.

they cuffed him took him
i was his right hand

he looked only at me when he said it.
he knew i knew
he was telling the truth.
he never cries.

i didn't want to go on without him
but time does not pause so you can catch
your breath—
the days dragged me by the hair,
snot nose, bloody knees, a feral left hand
and no one to tag in.

we never played as children again

## Lost Seed: An Abecedarian for Fatherless Daughters

A man did not father us. The daughters of no man, sailing without
ballast, use mirrors as maps, try to match our faces to pattern-less shadows.
Chest stabbed by the dagger of absence—morphing us superhuman.
Daughters of no man invest an eternity praying for lovers with stone hearts to
enliven but dead rocks pound love into no one. Knotted and lumped up,
fatherless daughters marry ghosts. i was engaged to an ocean wave, my lover is
gone now; left me, dissolved in the water. My sister's the wife of the wind.
Her first husband was a solar eclipse. We birthed every demigod in existence.
Invincible but it stings, having our nuclei pinched when we're tortured and
jinxed by witnessing a father press a shiny kiss on his baby girl's forehead—
killed and reborn with this solstice, surviving by eating our tails
like the serpent; grateful for the full stomach. It's a prude and common
misconception that daughters of no man become rebels/ strippers/ toxic/ or
never settle/ because of how seldom we meet our fathers—some are lucky
or sometimes unlucky (not yet a teen/ a virgin/ he called me a slut). Our
pain isn't always for pleasure—it's the opposite. Nevertheless, we give
quietly, it's our default superpower. Ripping the shirts off our backs,
ripping the skin, gifting the bone and the marrow, never expecting a
single thing back. Self/sacrifice like it's normal because we're indigenous
to a world all-maternal, universal holders of wisdom and light. Mother made
us unequivocally humble. Braving storms, lost, alone, we still smile at rainbows.
Voyagers searching for one thing, conquering everything else on the way.
We—lost seeds—grow in whatever dirt we land in. Abandon and kill us/ the
X-chromosome is resilient. The sacred feminine resurrected & rebraided in the
Y-chromosomes of our children. It is written; women will rebuild the planet as
Zion, restoring our very own image so the world will no longer be motherless.

## The Night i Watched my Twelve-Year-Old Brother Get Cuffed & Taken from our Home, Tearing Up, Saying: "i Didn't Do It!"
### (Part 3)

i was ten and a half
when he escaped.

i learned listening

to my frightened mother on the phone
    *he kicked a guard in the face?*
    *Jumped out the third    the third-floor window?*
he got away barefoot, limping in the snow.

    With    every    declaration    carnival-colored
    hummingbirds    speared down my open mouth.
    Wings furiously fluttered    a million claps    propelled
    my chest upward.    i soared to the ceiling    matched the height
    of my smile.    A hybrid of fear & elation
    reverberated    through me.
    Of course he escaped.    he would be the one
my legendary brother, *Elegua.*

Before hanging up
mother agreed to call the police if he came home

and after    months    of hiding

he did.        She did.

That night
they took him again.    Cuffed him    again.
    he just wanted a night home.
his eyes    two filled fish bowls    unspilled.

If he could just tag me in.

# Without Grammar

our elementary public school aint teach no grammar
                                              thank God the universe dont abide
by NYC zipcode zones and poverty lines
                              in the beginning   all poets      were illiterate

            on clear nights   id write    under the gray glow of a   one eyed black
                      *my wack ass teacher warned me to just write*      the moon

our elementary public school thrived
                            making sure born writers remained wild
brutal fist fights with muses
                        produced big banged bursting poems full of blood salt & mucus
the words had to get out
                      like music or violence    possession dont ask permission
one way or another
              these muthafucking words got out

we never called our elementary public school     grammar school

cause it aint teach no grammar
                     kids got all the way through high school
and aint never heard of no oxford comma
                                *is that some rich people shit*

chop the legs off little girls & boys chasing destinies of creating poetry since the age of four
      fence birds from flight    flowers from full bloom
                                         but the raven or the rose
                                                gonna do what it do
we literary convicts   dont give a fuck   spit wrong language   make it up   fire it off flaming hot
tongues    words that sprout tastebuds on bones   *spicy*    feel it in your whole body
                                                    only to be copied     un cited

and our lawless words     that sing swinging first     that dont ask permission

      that Richter when spoken     that slap pass the margins

                                                          wont be awarded no honors

                       Goddamn gatekeepers

# The Night i Watched my Twelve-Year-Old Brother Get Cuffed & Taken from our Home, Tearing Up, Saying: "i Didn't Do It!"
## (Part 4)

we were teens when he
came home, a blood stained sun, no
birds left in the sky

# She Looks Like Nirvana
*Based on Kenny Rivero's "Lunar Map" painting, oil on linen, 2022*

A girl grows
out bloomed youth big gold hooped bamboo ear lobes
false lashes fall off third eye sly self cut bangs do hide

A girl grows
out loud fast towns *a-yo Ma* train rides tough
crowd nickeled dimes rough mood schools school *We* still real cool

A girl grows
out one size fits all tamed dull uniforms
bobby pins hair ties roped wild curls forced down do bust out

A girl grows
out worn down buttoned up school blouse tight mouth
one lid long blink fold neck closed chokeholds with slick smiles

A girl grows
gagged gasps air juxtaposed green thumbs makes some
woke nights gets it wrong breaks rules one open eye still cute

A girl grows
family trees out timb boot sweat gene pools
undo dads death clone big bros farm grown from sole to soul

A girl grows
alone        And on God
a girl grows        her own

# What a Pretty Little Girl

*What a pretty little girl, can I touch her*
*hair? Pinch her cheeks? Kiss her head?*
*Can I hold her? Kiss her tummy?*
*Make her laugh?*

    Fingers tickle.

it never ends

In the bathroom stall. On the playground.
In the yard. The water park. Behind the slide.

    Fingers fiddle.

less polite

In the pool, held underwater, as grown-ups talk
stopped on a walk, *say hello*, swooped onto his lap
leg pushed & pressed on something hard as they chatted.

But when momma asks, *has anyone touched you*
*there?* Trapped in momma's stare
the pretty little girl is confused because every time

she was there.

## As You Slept

Those Fall mornings
                      with my head on the windowpane
i cradled myself against the world's bosom. Then would turn
my back to the cracked window, let the breeze braid my hair.
The air fed my belly for breakfast, prepared me for school
so you could sleep Mami. Don't worry. You need your rest.

i cleaned the house,
                  did the laundry; for dinner, buttered
the last of the bread. In a silver pot with salt and warm water,
i soaked his foot, removed the cast and we soaked it good, like
they said, every day. Until the bullet that ricocheted into his
heel seeped out, and it did Mami. Maybe i'll be a doctor one
day. And the exit wound left on your other son's leg isn't fatal,
Mami. Your kids are resourceful. One is in jail but your kids
aren't dead. we can take care of each other, Mami. Please.
Rest.

As you slept, i didn't miss you
                        Mami. i know that place must
be better than this. Did those medicaid doctors prescribe all
this dreaming? Are you to capture your monsters while sleeping
to store in those empty pill bottles—why don't you throw them
away? The school asked again what you do for a living, i said
you work overtime fighting the urge to stop living. Busy dizzied
from when your past poses as present and you can't tell the
difference. i warned them not to disturb you Mami, cause you
need your rest.

In our shared bed,
                i'd tuck my foot underneath your warm body
hoping to link into your dreamspace. i wanted to see for myself,
what in your sleep keeps you wandering. Why do you awaken
exhausted. Then finally, with one eye closed to see better, i peeked
through their bullet-holes and found you Mami. Saw you, so pretty,
wearing bright red. Hair done, make-up to match, in those scuffed
dancing heels you never actually wear. Your laughter sounded like
glory, lips curved upward like arrows. My rainy eyes clouded the
window to the tiny universe where you're happy and awake. It's ok
Mami, as you slept, we took care of the
                            rest.

## The Real Miracle

It was that time of the month. i bled
into a lake for seven days
filled it with jellyfish. And

a man came, known for his game and gifts
of gab; the savior type, and i wanted saving.
He was in town for a wedding. A sweet-talker
told me i taste like wine.

Later that night i crashed the wedding at the lake.
To this day no one can tell me whose wedding
but it was a hell of a party.

When the wine ran out, my sweet-talker told them
to serve the lake water.
                                They guzzled it.
Mesmerized, they asked him:
        *How?   How'd you turn this water into wine?*

        *Oh. It was Miracle,* he said.

But that's not how it was written.
And everyone misunderstood.
*Miracle* is my name.
He was referring to me.

# To Deify a Roach: An American Horror Story
*Dedicated to my brothers/ my guerrero's/ D, K, & G*

Because there weren't any fireflies in the hood
as a child i imagined roaches were angels on a
mission. To save lives, they'd crawl into the mouths
of the chosen. Initially i found them disgusting.

They'd infest my Fruity Pebbles cereal. i'd pluck
them out—loved the sound of the homerun pop
when fingernail flicked their fat hollow bodies.
They survived the end of the world—so it wasn't

the end of the world. i knew the gods would be
pleased knowing i could see angels in roaches.
Eventually i became ill and broke out in rashes.
If this was a test, i passed it. i'd be just like Job

from the bible. Except i had no wealth to be stripped
of, no pride to call sin. A good citizen. Then one day
a toolbox of crime was left on our doorstep, inscribed
*paradox*. Hoping to fix things, what curious child

wouldn't pick it up? Instead it morphed the drug
dealers & murderers into my young brothers: *Elegua,
Chango & Ogun.* Toy guns became real guns, kids
who couldn't get new shoes or lunch, books or coats,

got semi-automatic weapons on their own. Kids who
could barely read or count suddenly ran labs, modified
molecules of white rocks; became botanist breeding
cannabis hybrids. We were hexed by American deception.

And i, a prepubescent *Oshun,* prayed to angelic waterbugs
for help. i wanted to manifest all our freedoms but just
sobbed *fuck the polic*e—a torch song clutched in my lungs.
i watched my Orishas walk cuffed, lined & chained into the

courts of 100 Centre Street, New York. i thought we consumed
enough roaches to protect us from these devil's Armageddon
but my brothers were reduced to 12/14/16 year old super
predators, sucking on thumbs, three strikes and auctioned to

prisons up north. These magistrates game with fake crowns
& real bars. The 1994 new age evil Crusades killed or caged
our loving warriors. By 1995 i was alone. My brothers were
gone, along with all the little boys i'd known growing up.

Fathers/uncles/sons: locked up or shot. us little girls were
left on the block unprotected for cops to pick up & try to fuck
in the back of police wagons—and all praise went to Clinton
and the nefarious Giuliani for cleaning the city up. And i won't

tell you what they do to little gods in Spofford, won't tell you
about the adolescents at war in Rikers C74. Or about my
beloved brothers' broken ribs, multiple stab wounds, burned
toes, cracked skulls, stomped-out teeth, scars from forehead

to jawbone. i won't tell you about teenage *Chango* and how
grown men stomped the life out of him over fruits that he
stored. Woke up days later chained to a bed inside the ward
with a different face than before. i won't tell you how the

guards left *Ogun* in chains and proceeded to use sticks, fists,
boots and mace. Sent him to a cell full of his enemies, kept
him chained, let them carve & stab him as they pleased.
i inhaled a bottle of pills to stop suffering. Selfish & dumb,

generic Tylenol does nothing. Then finally, my brother *Ogun*
was released. That day, i came home and found him asleep.
i tiptoed in to wish him sweet dreams but he's forgotten he's
free, punches me so hard my head hit the ceiling, chest caved

in, i struggled to breathe. But i forgave him before i dropped
to the floor, before he rushed over apologizing in horror
and before i could sob, he told me crying was for suckas
and it wasn't allowed. i hushed, neck clutched, tears

swallowed, frown fixed. i pretended to be   as tough as him.
I   rose   and fixed us   some   infested   Fruity Pebbles cereal

and that's when   I   realized

roaches were just roaches

and no one's   coming   to   save   us.

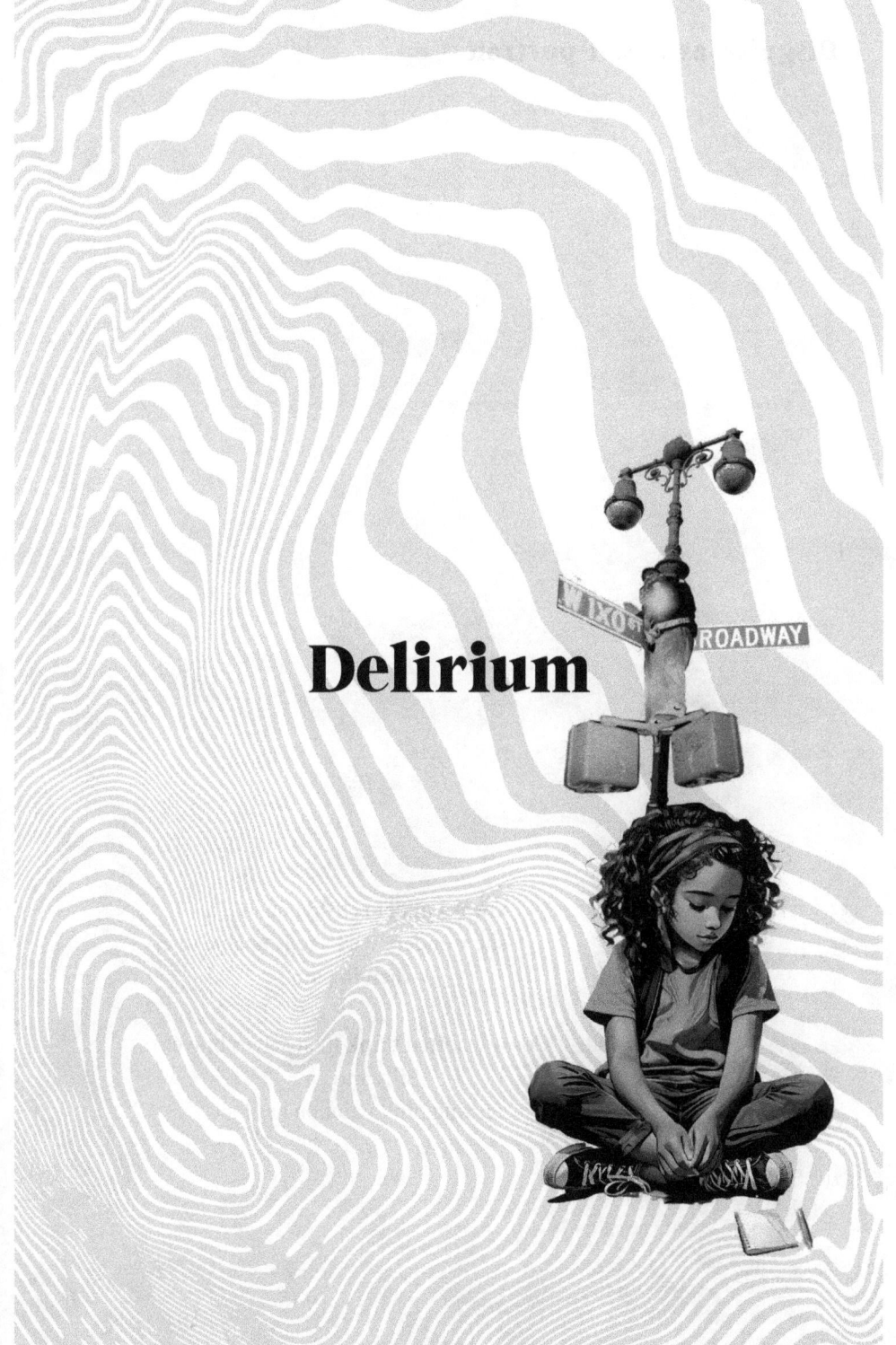

## Disguise as a self-portrait

 

 

always under self-hypnosis
she wonders why she is unable to cry
when in pain

Cowards often think themselves brave
Silly girl
smiling pink paint on her face

fake

safe

# 100 Centre Street, New York: Criminal Court

> *numb enough to know,*
> *the temperature at which no bird*
> *can thrive—Timothy Donnelly*

I hate that we don't need directions

I remember
      we walked there, the way I imagined the animals did—
orderly, fearful.    It is the opposite of Noah's Ark.
Instead of refuge, it delivers captivity. Instead of
salvation, destruction. Commanded there
not by angels, not to be spared judgment.

We walked there off the Franklin Street train station,
brown boys in borrowed slacks and button-down
shirts, scared to death, hoping they're not kept
in *The Tombs* and get to go home.

We walked there the way I imagined the animals did—
prayers packaged in throats like contraband poorly
hidden but undetectable by search. Instead of two
of each animal saved, a single group damned.
Here, a flood of women & men place punishment,
I fear this water.

      When my brother was sentenced to 25 years
I remember
      the feeling of drowning, gagging on adrenaline,
      not a lifeboat in sight. His eyes pulsing, he said nothing.
      From here there was no turning back.

      Armed with umbrellas to battle tsunamis, my best friend
      and I, age 14, skipped class to take the stand—
      our honest testimony made no difference in the end.

Is the opposite of a raven a dove? Or is it a tree
in this upside-down wrecked ark?

# Survivor's Guilt: A Villanelle
### *for the family members of the incarcerated*

> *"You're a Caribbean woman. You can't be without tribe."* —Willie Perdomo

I can only whisper this to you:
I've been called a survivor. It's a lie.
I've died 2,920 times. It's the truth.

I reanimate in *Sing Sing Correctional Facility*, visit siblings, play it cool.
I buried my heart—my mouth/ the tomb. Gagging on life
I can only whisper this to you.

I skinned my tongue razor-thin/ licked life out of the girls of my youth.
I can't bear their nostalgia. For each day my brothers served time
I've died 8,395 times. It's the truth.

I forgot, my wired bra lit the alarm/ my body searched in a room.
I pretend it's ok/ they all pretend too. Can't speak aloud/ I tried
I can only whisper this to you.

I can't cry at goodbyes. *Don't make it worse*: Mother's rule.
I can't avoid home, don't pop pills, do fly high. Without my beloved tribe
I've died 13,140 times. It's the truth.

   Visit prisons, grip, and gift our vocal cords like bouquets of bloodroot.
   Guilt-ridden for wishing *they're better off dead*—my spine/ my noose.
   This can only be whispered to you:
   *No one survives this.    It's the truth.*

## Love Like New York City Trees

Of all things    we take after New York City trees—
trees framed in gray, piss-stained cracking concrete
sidewalks    poorly bleached    tiny tectonic plates
crashing in heat around us. We fools in full foliage falling
in love coloring summer.

As quickly as green becomes yellow
yellow becomes fungus
summer fall winter    the sun rarely visits
love loses shimmer
and you say to me    you didn't sign up for this—yet still,
I pledged to ripen then rot    obediently
with you.

We grew in this street. Twig tips first kissed
between tenement buildings—cars honked
in celebration. Branches stretched in every
direction, some broken by erosion/ weathering/
the weight of tossed $54.11's/ or just superintendents.
Summer has come    & now I find myself alone,
rooted next to a stump.

# Pep Talks: A Hood Girl Goes to College

*Sis, maybe they had
better schooling—this don't make
them smarter than you.*

*Sis, it's ok you
pronounced 'ask' like 'axe,' they
can't say your sweet name.*

*Sis, don't listen to
professors, you're a poet.
So what if you can't*

*recite the sonnets
of Paradise Lost by heart,
they can't recite the*

*Ten Crack Commandments
by Biggie Smalls. Can stand on
Mammon—still ain't tall.*

*There is no shame, Sis
your words were birthed listening
to mothers' proverbs.*

*Worshiping authors
ain't a prerequisite, Sis
for writing poems.*

*One could memorize
every song ever composed—
still can't sing a note.*

*Sis, you been at this
game for years, the last hell made
you an animal.*

*Sis, this a new type
of pandemonium—new
rules, new manual.*

*Sis, you survived worse
things. Remember, they don't have
half the heart you do.*

*Sis, maybe they had
better schooling—this don't make
them smarter than you.*

## Sangana: A Good Girl Disease

A clown refusing to be made a fool
suffers
      great aggravation.
 Diluting in constant circus     she is
      a watercolor portrait
left in the rain.

She swallows iron nails to keep from
      speaking.
Told to play her role     the good girl listens
      despite internal bleeding.
She bothers no one
      won't inconvenience
and becomes a perfect home
      for triumphant demons to settle in.

 She gets a job cause "Writers don't make money"
      Still pretty poor, she draws iambic
pentameter anonymous
      on corporate bathroom stalls.

To endure slapstick routines
      she overdoses    on placebos,
over the counter and corner stores,
      numb
taking shots—rum/ cameras/ slaps/ slurs/
      Novacaine/ folded over/ or on her back—
she takes them all,
              except her own.

      Well behaved,
she chases the high
      of her self-prescribed
evanescent hallucination

only to learn:

            regret

                        cannot be

                                      sedated

# Pep Talks: A Hood Girl Dodging Assimilation

A fellow feminist questioned my commitment to the cause
    because I told her to *"suck my dick."*

A fellow Dominican told me I can't say the "n" word because our people
    never been through slavery, to which I said *"nigga what?"*

A fellow nonbeliever rebuked my need for prayer, preached the "right way"
    to be "Godless", to which I lit a candle to give light to my dead—

I need them near me now more than ever. After my blond-bluest-eyed-boss fired Griselda,
    she gazed into my eyes and declared the oddest assumption:

*"She's not like us. Her parents didn't go to college like ours."* Hiding my surprise, I realized,
    my disguise is working well. Is the real me that I kill   daily   truly undetectable?

I know one thing: when you speak their perfect English you're treated less like an animal.
    Belonging is exhausting.     Code switching is not assimilation     so I'm told.

Today, I deployed five different accents for five different situations
    and forgot how I behave when I get home.

# Nine Eleven Poem

I was in Brooklyn watching Manhattan burn
My morning bagel never made it out of its brown paper bag
    /it doesn't snow in September
I stood frozen on the promenade, clenched to the lip of the
gaping mouth of Brooklyn, facing not the river Jordan but
    the Hudson.   Everyone noticed no one
only devastation.
A cloud gliding toward us   flurried like snow but
    /it doesn't snow in September
The city's on fire. *Can a scorching sky crystalize autumn snow?*
Shadows wailing to my left, others buckled on my right.
    I see no one.
The city's on fire    the flurried snow got closer
but
    /it doesn't snow in September
I caught a large snowflake on my palm
it was not white,  not cold,  not moist,  not snow
    /it doesn't snow in September
though it creeps and falls like snow
in its dark warm dryness   ash   is everything snow is not.
    It dusted my clothes, slid in my mouth, up my nose.
The city's on fire   and I need to get home
to get home   I need to run toward the fire
    get through the fire
The fire is home.

The towers collapsing to powder
    /cremated    the ash blizzard in the eye of the storm.
Ashes falling/ folding on our heads/ cloaking bodies
into pillars of salt.   Hurrying forward   cause like Lot's wife
    we don't just turn our backs on New York.

Desiccated    I survived the long road home.
The September snow made an urn of my brown paper bag
    and bread into
               /stone

# Nine Twelve Poem
### *Dedicated to Reina Yolanda Burdie*

I was in Egypt nine months before the towers fell.
The people spoke to me in Arabic   *Roh Rohi*
I spoke back in English   so they called me "American"
      /I never called myself American.
            America never called me American - not without a hyphen.

My best friend Reina, doubles as a spirit guide.
I tell her   she is my peace,   the sister I never had,
to which she says   *Peace is thicker than Blood.*
Said the trip to Egypt would change our lives   and she was right.

After months of saving, we arrived just past midnight. Looking up,
my face was shoved between the long freckled legs of the Milky Way.
I saw night's uterus, its bright neurons singing, its translucent scrotum,
its organs living, a barely black skeleton stretching across a pulsating
skinless sky.   Beautifully broken, I wondered:
        *who'd stolen all of New York City's stars?*

On the first day of our tour   the world stopped.
All dropped to their knees in prayer   in unison.
This was not a drill. Worship in 9D, so potent I didn't understand
how in that moment that plot of land didn't break away and float
directly to the heavens.   I didn't let myself cry.   Holding it burned.

The pyramids of Giza are not hidden deep in the desert.
It's sectioned off like Central Park in a mini city of its own.
Hollywood hyped me up for a week's journey camel ride. Lies.
Stepping off the tour bus, I didn't mind the 8-year-old's running
up and picking our pockets in 76 languages. Dodging their quick
tiny hands I was breathless to be in the presence of geniuses.
They spoke to me in Arabic  /  but I spoke back in English

    *Where are you from?* They asked.
    *I'm Dominican and Saint Thomian.*

little faces, stumped...
>*but I was born in New York*

*Oh you're American?* They said.
My face, stumped...
>/I never called myself American.
>America never called me American.

Shopping at the market I let my peacock out.
After being repeatedly hustled, I learned quickly
how to bargain. Negotiating over a sterling silver letter-opener,
I accused the extra-large salesman of robbing us blind.
He insisted it was a good price. I insisted it was not.
>*Ladronaso! Reina, he's robbing us! Sir, you're robbing us!*
He flipped the fuck out. Slamming his hairy baseball-mitt-sized-fists
yelling in his beautiful accent:

# GET OUT YOU STUPID AMERICAN BITCHES!!!

>/again, with the "American"
I wanted to correct him   but instead        we ran for our lives.
>When we caught our breath   we laughed about it for hours.

Throughout the tour, everywhere we went we were mistaken
for one of them. The people spoke to us in Arabic and we were
flattered to be confused for magnificent Egyptians.
*Me*! King Hatshepsut. The Goddess Isis. A woman of the Nile

>***

In New York, on the days following 9/11, everyone hung American
flags from their windows     like a plea   in unison.
And everywhere I went    I was mistaken for one of *them*.
Waiting on a downtown train platform, I was called a *fucking terrorist*
by an extra-large white man who then spit where I was standing. A crowd
gathered salivating vengeance, full blown fury staring me down with hate
dilating their eyes. I wanted to tell them: *Peace is thicker than Blood*   I didn't
let myself cry.      Holding it burned.

And even when it could've saved me
I couldn't bring myself to say:
>*I'm American.    Even though I am.*

## When You Were Red

Because I can't live in pictures I reach
out to touch you. But I can't seem to find
today what the camera caught of us
yesterday. Where are you? My favorites
became favorites cause they reminded
me of you, but I don't see your colors
in all this gray. That's what gray does, you know,
breaks all the rules, leaves you afloat, confused
and you just can't tell your reds from your blues.
It's been two decades, the lights are dimmer
the stakes higher, the pot doesn't just simmer
these fucking flames now fly higher, they burned
away my eyelashes and I still can't
let myself cry. I've grown tired of climbing
to just fall and every time I stand tall
low ceilings remind me to crawl. So I
inhale this smoke and try to invoke the
physics of timing, the high sends me off
flying back to the time when you were red—
the tint of old childhood pictures taken
at Woolworths—eight by eleven, wood frame,
hanging on the wall in our living room.
When we were children, you were the best at
relieving stress, made everything easy
and effortless. Now you only call me
when you need something. You ask me to lie
and ride for you, visit and pay lawyers,
fool parole-borders, raise up your only
daughter, hold down your baby-mother then
run when the block heats up because I must
take care of our family tree stump. You
know it isn't your job to teach me first-hand
that life isn't easy because it never
was. That's what gray does. And I can only
see you in gray now. Lost in fogged-up rides
and weed clouds, caught up in big crowds that make
noise and speak loud but hear nothing and live
hard. So when I miss you now big brother
I prefer to look at the red color
of old pictures.

## *Stillmatic*

I was in the Bronx sacrificing doves—
(Baba would swiftly rip their heads off
like Challah bread breaking Yom Kippur)
by the mural of Fat Joe & Big Pun
where I came to pay blood in exchange for safety
    /his safety my legendary brother    *Elegua.*

All the way from Washington Heights, right off the Deegan
    he found me
as if the 160,000 miles of streets never distanced us.

    /I still don't know how    but he found me.

He hurried me inside his Range Rover, already high
off the nitrous oxide pumping out the speakers.
*Listen*, he said.   *It dropped today.*
He needed to be the |one| to deliver it to me, needed to bear
witness,   to be church for my monosyllabic prayer:   *Nas*

This is how he loves,   my legendary brother    Elegua.

His search for |me| rippled the gray out the block/ out the clouds/
out the clock—his ultraviolet light resurrected my childhood
suicides that I'd done to subside/ giddy little dead girls ascended
out the dungeons of my mouth   and joined us.

I rolled his blunt. He never let me smoke: *For your own good.*
He'd turn the speakers up/ paused/ rewind lines/ we zoned out.
Listened through sunset and nightfall to ethereal prophecy.
Nodded our heads until our thorn-crowns spun off
                                      into glowing disks.

I didn't know it then    that this day would be my favorite.
A holy day   all was forgiven

    /with the smell of dead pigeons still fresh on my fingers
        /Ashe

## Delirium

**104.4°F** - We fall asleep and wake up
like trees—we live half in light, half in
darkness, keening


**ΨOZ)** The Gods laugh, listening to us quote
all the things they did not say. Baffled
by the whale-like-groaning of our prayers
lacking the interpretation of the word *"forgiveness."*

...
*"You're only as good as the world
allows you to be"—laughed, The Joker*

**27m °F:** The fevered sun in all its glory is never out past curfew—
I'd like to meet its warden.

...
*Elegua is now serving sixteen years in federal
prison for selling weed. sixteen years—
there isn't poetry for this     only fever: 106°F*

**π.**
When traveling outer space one doesn't
encounter stars. Just floating rocks lost
falsely assigned some divine luminescence.

...
*A boy was just arrested on 145th Street for selling weed
not far from a coffee shop that sells coffee induced with
weed. The boy is brown, the coffee shop owner is not
but we already knew that     didn't we*

**π.** *continued*
The stars aren't already dead, they never
even existed. We've been catfished by the night.
Perhaps the light we see is our own reflection.
If so, we've been catfished by the light.

> ...
> When I was little, I learned chivalry
> from my uncle—high on cocaine, he shot himself
> in the palm of his hand to avoid killing his girlfriend
> during an argument. His blood flooded my apartment
> which I cleaned up. His scar healed in the shape of a
> rose.   A rose!  I used to think that was the craziest
> part of that story.        He was deported.

|X|
What pointless reconnaissance.

## PUBLIC SERVICE ANNOUNCEMENT:

> Tomorrow
> about half the continent
> will overdose
> on opioids

> we already knew that—silly me.
> Gods, forgive

# How To Break Your Mothers Heart

Mami, forgive me. I've forgotten all my scriptures
and I'm no different than when my prayers metered
my pulse. I tried retaining details of your favorite,
Psalms 37: 20-something: *the righteous will inherit the earth.*

Mami, like birds flying north, all the Saints have left us. Now
who can be anointed, who can earn Canonization under the
watch of the internet's all-seeing-eye? The unforgiving world
wide web broadcasts our sins      immortalized

Mami, I've grown impious despite your greatest efforts.
I thought I caught the holy spirit but it was just coronavirus.
I've tried to feed my faith outside religious sectors but found
zero eschatologists when searching *Linkedin* profiles.

Mami, I spent the night at church, and stayed well into
the morning dancing at *The Limelight*—a church converted
to a nightclub with pre-existing glory holes and absolution
garnished with lemon-peel-halos at the bar.

Mami, it's been decades waiting for *The Last Days*, I need *Him*
to deliver. I'll make it clap if Azazel can make it rain flaming
boulders from the sky, riding the seven-headed Beast we studied in
the bible—whenever you'd awaken from your medicated somber.

Mami, why did God create an angel with mental health disorders?
Abandoned, you aged out of the group home in Saint Thomas and
to avoid being homeless, you took a shoe, beat your head bloody
and unconscious then woke up in the hospital to a warm bed.

Mami, remember how you'd always tell me that you would've
killed yourself if you didn't find Jehovah? I'm grateful that your
faith has never faltered. Enjoy your promised paradise on earth,
God knows that you deserve it. Just wake me when it's over

cause this here is a special kind of torture and I'd much rather
burn than pretend all this is normal. Mami, I've lost all my religion
I'm still trying to be righteous but I'm a sinner—
                    roaches will inherit the earth.

## Blue Passport

It's that scent when a match burns off
an entire island on fire
                       extinguished
seconds before I stepped off the plane.
Inhaled burnt orange, soaked it on my tongue
and thought   *sulfur*:  the aftertaste
                  of French-kissing Mars

Immediately, I felt my skin glow,
felt the UV's alchemy convert iron cells   into gold.
Here, the sun is God's placenta; in utero, her rays plug
into my pores—a billion umbilical cords—feeding me
nutrients raw.

The view of this ocean is medicine
the portal of all life    clapping
dancing merengue
waving hello and goodbye
                  at the same time.

The air is clean in my nostrils   young,
moist, weightless
maybe released from a Ziploc bag
from the first ice age
              *am I breathing water?*

This breeze is vaporized serotonin, blowing
away all my worries. In the seconds I stepped off
the plane, unbeknownst to me, natives called me
by the name of their beloved martyred woman
warrior poet cacique king.

Finally     Ayiti

To no longer be   from somewhere   I've never been

## La Boca de Nigua
*From the Forever Island Documentary*

La Boca de Nigua sings of rebellion,
of the master's ashes plastered across this fallen finca de caña,
of caramelized flames dancing over the first sugar mill of the
Americas.

It sings, afro-indigenous-rituals, beating our hearts
pidiendo puertas abiertas a Papa Legba

The earth left testimony: bloomed Morivivi throughout the ruins.
Land has muscle memory.
Here, plants spasm in reaction, flinch post-traumatically to touch,
shies cause it remembers fire, hides cause it remembers blood.

Aquí, pelearon la primera rebelión.
con palos llamaron y bajaron a Papa Legba a cerrar el camino
de los demonios colonialistas de San Cristóbal.
Aquí, comieron fuego de Papa Candelo.
Aquí, se incendiaron y murieron.

The tongue of any land is a drum made of skins stretched
over hallowed wood; y con esta lengua sagrada hablamos
directamente con nuestros luases.
Palo: a call and response beyond the stars, it is how we bring
Ogún Balenyó to fight with us in times of war.

Listen to the trees, the throats of the center of the earth
screaming silence to quiet the chaos of the world.
El viento envuelto en las alas de los muertos volando al cielo.

Agua de Nigua, limpia el cuerpo. Santificadas sean las madres.
Las olas se doblan como niñas riendo. Un futuro divino despierta
con San Antonio de cabeza. Waters don't repeat past sins, push us
forward.

      Gracias a la misericordia.

# |Absolute Value|

I was in Staten Island/ bed-side to my grandmother's purgatory.
My mother's mother   screeching for days   on a hospital bed.
Already dying painfully   she was dropped   her leg snapped in 2 places
but staff didn't report it   left it untreated   to avoid a lawsuit. Her eyes
bloodshot   almost demonic   dying   not peacefully—but in   pure   fury.

                       This is not your typical *I love my grandmother* poem.
                       I hardly knew her    punched her in the face when I was 14.
                       I had only recently met her and she hit my mother.
                       It's inexcusable.  By far   my most infinite shame.

It was naive   but I waited    to hear the world stopped
after her last breath   waited for all to rise
and gather   silent    to acknowledge her passing.
She lived a whole wretched life—all Dukkha.
And isn't it cosmic law that life's to cycle   good *and* bad?
Hers was all Yin      zero Yang.

                       A pretty little girl    traded for a radio   married off at 14
                       to a man age 53.    At 15 she gave away her firstborn,
                       her pretty little girl,   to her wealthy sister-in-law.
                       She kept her other 4 children then was eventually
                       left widowed in *el barrio De Los Guandules*
                       *Dominican Republic* where cab drivers shiver
                       and only visit during daylight.

I waited  for the ceiling to crack    for a cliché light
for a baritone voice to announce   the cosmic malpractice
but the universe    didn't report it.

                       I lied.
                       This is an *I love my grandmother* poem,
                       an *I wish I was better to my grandmother*
                       poem. She was a fighter. I am proud.
                       I was too much of a coward to tell her "I'm sorry." Bed-side
                       I kept it knotted on a rock clotting in the bottom of my gut.
                       Mother's rule: *suck it up, don't make it worse*—is hard to unlearn

                       and then she died.

I just graduated college   and for months  I couldn't find a job.
My mother's mother    never liked me much   so I thought.
But even in agony  she asked daily if I had any luck finding work.
The day after she passed    I was hired on the spot.
I know that was her.    Beneath all the hurt   there was kindness
that I didn't deserve.

We spread her ashes in the Hudson, as she requested
but the moment we released them, a gust of wind
pushed her remnants in the opposite direction.
Even her last wish—rejected.

                            Is there a courthouse that holds the cosmos accountable?
                To petition a Dharma Habeas Corpus for her unnatural lengths
                in darkness?    No *otherworld* to command answers    as to why
                      why some people suffer so bad?     No place to file a claim
                              to correct the imbalanced mathematics
                                  calculate    the absolute value of
                                          |her life|

cause I need to know
                who got all her joy?

who can I see   about giving it back?

I need to ensure
                her afterlife    is glorious

# Pep Talks: A Hood Girl in Corporate America

### I

Britney never got the life stomped out of her in the schoolyard
as evidenced by the way she spews microaggressions without
squaring-up
    Rule 101:   never leave your guard down
    Rule 101a:  don't start nothing, won't be nothing
    Rule 101b:  if you gonna start something, square-up

In the seconds she rolled her eyes saying, "I swear, you people..."
I could've roped a handful of hair around my wrist then dragged her
backward and guillotined an open-hand karate chop to her trachea.
But not today. I tell myself:

> *sis, you must unlearn these things*

### II

Barbara believes the token-less are better suited for retail instead of the
executive conference room, potentially snatching *her* job. She wonders
what backdoor I crawled in from, finds ways to remind me I don't belong.
She questions my white-wash because of my water-cooler-talk about the
Jay Z and Mary J. Blige Hip Hop concert I attended over the weekend.
They talk about family getaways to the Hamptons. I never share about my
weekends in Coxsackie, Green Haven, or Sing Sing maximum security
prisons.    It makes her uncomfortable how comfortable I am in my skin.
> *She has no idea.*

Eating lunch, Barbara hears me mention my Ivy League alma
mater. She mutters, "Thank God for affirmative action..."
"What was that?" I say with a cold Mona-Lisa smirk on my face.
Barbara gulps a reply—
    "There's so much opportunity for education these days..."

I tell myself:    *she too must unlearn some things*

### III

These women terrify me though I don't show it. I know what they are
capable of. They've made frequent appearances in my life—the lady
shaped like a stuffed laundry bag who talked down to my mother
during our welfare appointment. The tired lady with stained teeth
at the front desk of the prison, huffing in annoyance, slamming papers,
regurgitating instructions, refusing to let anyone get a word in.

They never look you in the eye

*sis, you must let go of these things*

### IV

Bald-old-Bob called me into his office, asked me to shut the door.
Squinted his pale blue eyes and said:
         "Look   I'm just going to say it,   I think you're hot"
Bob never got the life stomped out of him    anywhere
and he's used this line before on twenty-something-year-old girls.
Corporate Bobs don't need to square-up. America is all the muscle
they could want. Calculating my hands' distance to every sharp object,
my face mean-muggin, I say, "Thanks, I think… my boyfriend would agree"
then unfolded my hands as if to say: anything else?

*sis, you can't call your big brothers to request a quick choke hold,*
*Tribe-less with no safety net   sis, you must unlearn these things*

(Rules If accosted by an office pervert:
- Look straight through his retina, telekinetically seize hold of his optic nerve.
- Do not blink, do not shake, do not sweat, do not gulp.
- Though you are scared, do not show it.
- Furrow your eyebrows to express 49% confusion & 51% violence.
- The farce confusion is an illusion: pretend to have misread the situation,
which provides him a safe out—otherwise, meet him with loud
furniture-rearranging face-biting bloody violence should he try it.
- While in silence adjust your stance shoulder width for balance.
- Do not speak, do not doubt, stare him down.
- Amp yourself up, slightly tilt your head, think things like
"I wish this mutha fucka would; dead-ass I'm bout to plunge
this fountain pen in the abyss of this bitch ass niggas eye…"

      - Then for his own good, telepathically project the playground rules:
          Rule 101a:  don't start nothing, won't be nothing
          Rule 101b:  if you gonna start something, square-up)

Bob grinned,   laughed it off   and told me to have a nice day.

I flashed a cold Mona-Lisa smile then walked off
(alone breathing blinking shaking gulping sweating renouncing God sick in a bathroom stall, wondering how does one square-up frozen from the feet up)

    *sis, don't unlearn these things*

          **V**

Alarm goes off. I sit up quietly sucking my teeth for twenty-five minutes straight
as my mother continues to sleep in the bed we share.
I wonder why it's called a glass ceiling when it feels more like drowning
in a fishbowl   smiling.    Always smiling.

    *sis,   you survived worse things*

## Rose was a rose was a rose

I know why the rose grew thorns.
Its stem adapted to man's hand
on its throat

For this reason, I hope little girls grow armed
with deadly toxins released by unwanted touches,
women's skin resistant to assaults of acid

We'll evolve with unbreakable ribs
Lips that shiv    Diamond-hard cheekbones
breaking the knuckles and wrists

of anyone who dares punch us
Labia made of two razored petals
for the unwelcome—

so        we        too
can       stay      alive
a         little              longer

## Emissaries and God Bodies

I'm not sure where it comes from
but I've seen it. Magnified

in the sunlight of a melodic moment
the stillness of a rock pulsating—

ripples sway the leaves of a small tree
as if passing a secret through movement.

In its special morning appearance
the crescent moon arching arabesque

pulls the wind I pushed out of my lungs
I'm not sure where it comes from

but I've seen, in a breath, death tear through
the skin of sky leaving only a body behind

# Fear of Water

## *The Raft of the Medusa*
### *Based on Theodore Gericault, Oil Painting 1818*

Is our entire journey   going to be like this?

Sail off,  meet disaster,  turn back   to more disaster
pyramids of disaster—difficult to dismantle
turn back   get here   turn back again
despair aboard despair

hope  hidden in the horizon   just over the bodies
cannibalized   to carry us there

# Dead President$

*I hope they assassinate him*

The daughter sighed to her elderly mother on the A train to 207<sup>th</sup> street. Sucking her teeth like a whip of wet Caribbean winds, the mother said

*Silly girl, they don't kill leaders for doing bad*
*They only get killed when they try to do good*
*The devil protects them*

The daughter replied
*I gotta write this down*

The mother proclaimed
*Make sure you write my name, A. Folin. So they come for me*

# Water Fear

**

On the guttered shore of a bleeding Broadway street corner
in the slums of New York's glorious Manhattan, I stand
wondering how we came to be stranded on this island's island,
circumferenced by thousands of exits—but oh how the tides
taunt and betray us

At red dawn, our black sun and incarnadine skyline clearly
outline all that is not meant for us—luxury buildings with
balconies that leisurely snort the clouds, zoned schools with
more books than cops and clean kid-filled-playgrounds that
don't get shot up. Venture to this bright part of town without
token security clearance, you'll be captured by navy-blue badged
currents and dragged out

Still, we swim down, self-taught and token-less, swim under
the red dawn, toward your yellow sun, chase dreams and drown

And if the waters don't kill us, we return clawing to our redlined
island of a street corner; deranged/ drenched/ coughing/ poisoned
with Hudson River sediments/ ossifying pain like pearls—our hearts
layered with nacre protect us from being crushed against the solid
white bedrock

# Ge-he-na

*Gehenna* - *a valley in Jerusalem. A biblical symbolic hell. A destination for the wicked.*

At the hotdog stand I remember how
much you hate ketchup—the large hermit crab
    that made a home of my chest crawls
out red from the mollusk shell under my ribs.
    When beckoned, it finds the innermost
raw flesh and gets to pinching,   scraping—

    claw caught and tugging on bone. Leaving
small lines carved on my skeleton—a count of
    all the days I miss you. This pain is now
citizen of my flesh. Thoughts of you my big
    brothers, call it to surface. Not thinking
of you, enrages it. I hunch over, agonize. Surrender

    to the scaring. Hold my breath like I've
been sentenced to live under the weight of three
    oceans, in Gehenna. Another hermit crab made
a home of my skull. Crawls out a pink-gray from the
    shell of my head, pries my eyes open to the
reality that you no longer have freedom. To accept that

    you're caged. Caged—a thought too demented
to be housed in my head, I shake it away. Your decades
    in prison prove I'm not as good a sister as I
thought, as I promised to be: *I'll be there for you.* You
    fed me, starving—fixed Tang drinks and syrup
sandwiches. You always defended and loved me.

When that boy followed me home, you ran
down wearing only sneakers and boxers, with a double-
    headed sledgehammer extending from your arm
like *Chango's* double-edged axe, you questioned him and
    then proceeded to knock his teeth out. It's been over
a year since I visited any of you. I'm trying to be a mother

    now so I can name my son after one of you. I've
become a scavenged whittled husk haunted by not doing
    right by you. I hold my breath often and brace
myself for the clawing. Pray for it to pass. You should
    know I can't stomach my reflection, so I dive
under it, under water, into my own Gehenna.

# *Born in Babylon Both Nonwhite And Woman*

### 1. Why anyone could take years to disclose rape or sexual assault
*For Anita Hill & Christine Blasey Ford*

Ever watch the pretty colors of blood
blending with semen & soap & water
cascade over bruises shaded like sunsets
on billowing battered thighs clouded by
tears & terror pooling in the shower?
—sort of looks like rainy autumn.
Ever wondered if it's possible for the bones
of your groin to fracture? Ever convince yourself
this amount of soreness is normal    until you sit
and it hurts so bad it knocks the life out of you?

because it didn't happen to you
if you never accept
        it happened to you

**2. Exclusion Criteria**

When the people of West Africa were dying
from the Ebola virus, MSF sent humanitarian men
to help the crisis. Instead, these men bartered
medicine for sex—targeted young girls who lost
their parents. They employed the good old Babylonian
slogan: exploit the problem/ never solve it.

These women said #metoo but no one listened.
When someone finally exposed this. No one listened.
When the article came out. No one listened.

>    Who will tell them
>            their truth isn't trending
>    Who will tell them
>            there isn't a hashtag for them

## 3. For the women in office who voted kavanaugh onto the supreme court

You must ask yourself     how deep is your penis
envy? How badly do you want *in* on the boy's club?
Did your mothers not teach you of the sweet
nothings boys whisper that leave you barefoot and
heartbroken and without constitution?

We see you     pimping your phantom-suffrage;
covert operatives working to maintain the privileges
of your white sons, fathers, and husbands.
We see you     reinforcing Babylon's falling walls
using our freedoms as mud and our rights as rods.

Faux feminist sellouts, fickle backstabbing bitches,
elected on false pretenses of sisterhood and equity.

Don't you see     so many of us don't have a seat
at that table. Do you expect us to eat whatever falls
on the floor? You'll say we're all eating the same
food and should be grateful     to eat at all.

Don't you see     we needed you to show up.
These roads were hand-carved with fingernail tiles
stretching for miles  and they've reversed us back
to the start.

And I don't give a fuck if these poems are too preachy
fuck poems   fuck craft    fuck pink pussy hats
fuck it all

I hope you drown in this blood

# Percussion

*To speak the word:    Percussion*
*notice how it requires breath— exhaled.*

*Close your eyes.*
*Say it slowly*

*see how it commands   puckered lips*

*an open mouth   now sshh   then*

*smack the back of your tongue lightly clasping your throat—exhale*

*then lick   the back of your teeth   with the tip*
*of your tongue*

*end with gentle suction.*

*To speak the word:    Percussion*
*simulate the slow seduction*
*of a deep kiss.*

*Close your eyes*

*feel the word in your whole mouth*

*Say it slowly*
*again*
*tilt your head*
*say it slower*
*choke a bit*
*drag the lick*
*play with it*

*To speak the word:    Percussion*

*it costs the air in your lungs*
*emptied*
*from the chest,   requires you*
*to mimic the moment before death— exhale*

*—be free*

# Nirvana Sky

      She   is a prayer    morphed

To reach her, I slayed three dragons
stole their depth of lungs
inhaled the galaxy in its entirety
      swallowed planets whole
until there was nothing
            but a path.
To reach her
     I left the world.

Kept only the pure pieces of myself
drained my blood   replaced it with music
shattered my bones thinking in high octaves
skin respun from threads of sound

     I traveled
in a reverse figure 8 pattern
to the cubed root of a future sun
   then
dove into a space smaller than a quantum wave.
To fit   I had to strip   lose it all.
Evolve backwards
beyond my spirit form—
         became blacker than Kali

and found her

     held her
in the spiraling song that knit my womb.
Bigger than ever, I regurgitated heavens earths and
moons—hailed myself human and kept her flame
inside me.

        They say daughters are a sign of great Karma
         from a past life.   I know I don't deserve her.
        My Nirvana Sky—curly crown and almond eyes.

        She is my extinction and resurrection.

          She   is a dream    morphed

# Stormborn
### *For Nirvana & Zion*

### I

Nirvana arrived on a Tuesday afternoon in April as lightning-sirens
whipped clouds into tsunamis swollen purple. The heavens awakened louder
than we'd ever heard before—a standing ovation, as if angels jumped on nimbus
towers and sent my baby girl off to me in thunderous rounds of applause.

Naturally magnetic, like bone alloyed of rare earth, but she despises
the orbiting attention—too often missed by the evil eye. She tries
to fight it, shrinks her shadows but her shine and name won't let her hide.
She's too young to manage magic from being born of storms.

### II

Zion arrived on a Wednesday afternoon in March as a blizzard rendered
New York City shut. A crystal veil of winds and cotton blanket icy static fogs.
My baby boy ceremoniously delivered to me from cloud to ground behind a
purdah of blazing snow.

He stops to ask me why one day I'll have to die. Thinks too far, loves the cold,
prepares for fire, hates change he can't control. Like the snow, he's silent, beautiful,
and full of hope. Always melting, crying, ideas wild, irrational. Anxious thoughts
with wind speeds off the charts—his mind inhabits a three-hundred-year-old
storm.

### III

My snow. My thunder. My son. My daughter.
Of course you aren't normal, the sky crashed down during your births.
I see you search for quiet and I hope one day you'll find it
though it's not that kind of world.

## Eat Their Young

It's true. If the father is left in the cage
he'll eat his young.
I've seen it.
And because I've seen it, first hand,
—the gore, blood, scattered bits—
with my own childhood
hamsters,
I should've known better

Worse even, hand first
my father left   his gluttonous ghost
gnawed away pieces of me
mauled my body's most inconvenient
corners   corners I try to fill, fall
out
not enough of me left   to hold things in
place
When healing amputations, nothing grafts
flesh better than your own flesh
but ghosts are skinless / so I'm half synthetic
and always peeling

Hardly human, my father's a monster
the worst kind, metaturnal—haunts
in darkness & daylight

So when I watched it happen to my young
I should've known better.
I should've protected my children.
Should've pushed him out of our cage sooner or
at least screamed, clouding the glass cage
until it burst into rain
    But I didn't            because
humans don't do that I thought
    I thought
humans don't do that

## For The Days I Don't Love NY Because I Missed My Train, Was Already Late, And Then Gave My Orange Juice Away

New York was pulled from a Gothic novel

The bland night sky painted
by an insecure part-time artist
(with a catatonic muse)
who later found success in law

Its sun is a fluorescent bulb
poorly manufactured. The rain isn't rain
just a dirty leak & when exposed to skin
requires a tetanus shot

The hot garbage piled on street corners
blights pedestrian tongues & nostrils.
Inhale lunch on a park bench, ignore three
hungry homeless men, pass time watching
pigeons with switchblades battle rats
over discarded pizza—to the death
                */there's no church in the wild*

Walk slow enough, get stopped & instructed to
fuck your mom, kill yourself, or quit your job
*tell your boss you're too much of a bitch ass to
get to work, stay off these streets, go home*—by
someone from Kansas who's been here too long

It's considered a lucky day when the infamous
belligerent lady preaching on the train is
confronted by an even more belligerent lady
on the train, screaming what you wished to say

Everyone loves New York
New York loves no one.
A barren gray island on stilts
with fingernails painted black
and far too much makeup

The streets are not made of gold.
The gold is not made of gold.

## Dear Lover

Because you asked
why I think we are on this earth
and I replied, "to eat mangoes."
Why cosmic beings specifically choose to be
Earthlings is because of mangoes.

To eat a ripe Mango it   commands   all your attention.
It is urgent.   demanding.   you must focus else it slips.
It bursts hyperactive once you crack into its skin
move fast    contort your spine and neck   rush, suck
the juices as it escapes out your desperate slurping mouth.
Quickly wipe the nectar off your frantic lips, catch as much
as you can with your tongue as it drips between fingers and
streams down your arms   losing momentum   slowly
rain-dropping    off your elbow.
Your face a glorious orange wet. Hairs stuck between teeth.
Hands sticky sweet, tainted bright and quickly drying.
Eating a mango is smelling a mango and in smelling a mango
one gets high off the mango until all you can think of is mangoes.
It is void of half-stepping. Invoking all senses directed into that single
dedicated moment         if you are fully to enjoy it.

Just like life.

But because you asked
And because you asked
This is how
I want you
To eat
My vulva

## *Gold Griot*
### Based on Jean-Michel Basquiat Oil on Wood Painting, 1984

Griot, as kin i stand before you. This skin i wear is just the soot
from shadows i cannot live without. i see your naked winking face,
a bone-like-black traced in opal orbs. Thanks to you we half-know
Africa as root. Griots, poets, artists hold all that's known and breed
it beautiful. Turn wooden tombs into golden rafts, sail the universe.
With all you know, Griot, we don't bury you in dirt. You're buried
in the ribs of trees and in return the trees preserve sacred memories.

Transfer knowledge inside seeds whose amniotic sacs make for the
sweetest cunning fruit—cause history is known to famish our truths.
For symbiosis, Baba taught me how to serve our ancestors drinks.
He said swoosh the gin inside my mouth, mix it up with spit, blow
it out my lips and they'll taste the oral lexicon absent from my DNA.
Custom-make medicines, send lessons packaged in rain. When crossing
planes of past & present we communicate through water, blood or grain.

You were my father once, Griot. My mother. My Baba, teacher, lover.
i am Griot too—eating fried pork shoulder soaked in citrus juice. i try
to remember half-remembered things. i see our image in rusted mirrors,
fight to fill the blanks. Halo me a hero? i have your favorite gin. Save
us from the ruse of the diasporic-fugue? Please feed me everything you
know. You won't catch me repelling ghosts. i see your hand extending out,
as i scratch my way inside to escape this world and hold: the great, the gold   Griot.

## Desahogarse: Undrowning (Suéltame Sataná)

*I wasn't gonna tell nobody    but I couldn't keep it to myself*
sang the choir    exposed my guilty pleasure    my penance & consecration:
writing poems    that greet you
pussy first.        Oh how the world prefers my trauma meager
kept a secret    fully clothed.

I swear    I wasn't gonna tell nobody    but    shared    suffering
dilutes suffering    and I couldn't keep it to myself

I wish I could    sell it.    profit.    as I've been accused
but damn macroeconomics and its theory of natural limits
*my* pain isn't special    in a saturated market    it cannot be sold
cause everybody got their own

But Ooooh    how their sour tones change    if an author    appropriates
my pain.    Tells my story for me.
They'll award that man a    Pulitzer.    money.    tenure.    fame.
Praise how well he captured    the woes of the    shipwrecked
ghetto girl    who fought incubus pythons
at the bottom of the Hudson    and lived to hide the scars
inside a pearl    that formed between her thighs

But no    so they fully cringe    call my poems    porn
because they greet you    pearl-less    immodest
pussy first

It's sin.    and soulless.    to be beaten and told    your screams
are just for show    (and I wasn't even gonna tell nobody)
but like Redemption song    *my hand was made strong*

    Poets write pain

   cause when you call a demon by its name

you command it

*I hope the exit is joyful*

*and I hope never to return.*

—*Frida Kahlo*

*All water has a perfect memory
and is forever trying to get back to where it was.*
—Toni Morrison

## Fear of Water

Since Water has

true memory, could it be before

gravity perfected its hold, the ocean's other-half rose

in high tide and unintentionally jumped up too far, floated off

and got stuck? Maybe balled itself up just as it froze, rocks and all,

forming into the orbiting moon? Could it be, they are spinning in an eternal

torture, unable to forget that they were meant to be one body of water; broken

and unwhole without the other, incapable of letting go of the pure form they once

shared? They will forever magnetically pull for one another, stopping at nothing,

even if it births Earth's destruction. They will fight to reunite or will drown the

whole world trying, or maybe ice the hydrosphere over, slowing us down, un-

aligning the solar system, causing planetary collisions; shipwrecked,

deliriously melding into the furnace sun, killing us all, until

they become one again. Would it be wrong

to root for them?

## Fear of Water

Almighty Water, the pure most
powerful of elements: solvent, transcendent,
and immortal; with its ability to resurrect and reinvent
itself  without religion, God's existence, magic, or the need
for human worship—it is proof that reincarnation is just nature, neither
miracle nor myth, nor paired with karma nor sin, nor enlightenment. Even all-
knowing Water, with its capacity to  heal,  cleanse,  disappear, then condense,
always returns  falling  as it rains again. Glorious Water, showing the ever-full Sun
how  life  requires so little fire— even  Water  suffers   loss —stuck and hopeless in
its pursuit, how it gets close but never close enough to touch   its first love. Doomed
to watch the moon   slowly   fall   apart, then pull itself  full  each month,  just to
restart.  I think of this when hitting   head-first  crystal ceilings, or when missing
my incarcerated brothers and sisters—that  life  by nature  isn't fair    and death
offers no guarantees   *all*   of our ancestors are still here.  Our spirits caught,
looping in liquid, imprisoned in the memory of this iron rocks life-giving
force. Therefore, my greatest fear of all   is that we won't return
to stars or have our  souls   released  beyond  because
this blue globe   is  inescapable
for  us.

*All water has a perfect memory*
*and is forever trying to get back to where it was.*
        *—Toni Morrison*

## Notes:

- **Shipwreck Poem** – after *Monsoon Poem* by Tishani Doshi.

- **Almost** – (ICE) U.S. Immigration and Customs Enforcement. (ERO) Enforcement and Removal Operations.

- **Lost Seed...** – after Natalie Diaz's poem *Abecedarian requiring further examination of Anglikan seraphym subjugation of a wild Indian rezervation*

- **As You Slept** – after *Those Winter Sundays* by Robert Hayden and *Unemployed Mami* by Willie Perdomo

- **Pep Talks: A Hood Girl Dodging Assimilation** – language borrowed from *The Bluest Eye* by Toni Morrison

- ***Stillmatic*** – title borrowed from Nas album *Stillmatic* and language borrowed from lyrics by AZ, from the song titled *Phone Tap* "straight from Washington Heights, right off the Deegan"

- **Rose was a rose was a rose** – title after language borrowed from the poem *Sacred Emily* by Gertrude Stein

- ***The Raft of the Medusa*** – based on Theodore Gericault's painting, *Le Radeau de la Meduse 1818*

- **Dead President$** – title borrowed from lyrics by Nas from the song, *The World Is Yours*

- ***Born in Babylon Both Nonwhite and Woman*** – title borrowed from Lucille Clifton's poem, *won't you celebrate with me*

- ***For The Days I Don't Love NY...*** – language borrowed from Jay-Z and Frank Ocean's lyrics from the song titled *No Church in the Wild*

- ***Gold Griot*** – based on Jean-Michel Basquiat's 1984 painting *Gold Griot* (acrylic and oil stick on wood) - also includes a quote by Bob Marley: "Africa is root"

- ***Desahogarse...*** – language borrowed from The Abyssinian Baptist Choir song titled *Said I wasn't Gonna Tell Nobody* and the song by Bob Marley *Redemption Song*

# Acknowledgments

- Currents: Writing The Land Anthology: *Shipwreck Poem*

- Forever Island Documentary: *La Boca de Nigua*

- "I'm Not a Painter, I Just Brush Alot" by Kenny Rivero & Charles Moffett Gallery: *She Looks Like Nirvana*

- "I'm Not a Painter, I Just Brush Alot" by Kenny Rivero & Charles Moffett Gallery: *Fear of Water 1*

- The Common Magazine: To Deify a Roach: *An American Horror Story*

- The Common Magazine: *Fear of Water 2*

- The Common Magazine: *Nine Twelve Poem*

- The Common Magazine: *Almost*

- Smithsonian Museum 9/11 Archive: *Nine Eleven Poem (video)*

- Released as a Spoken Word single across all streaming platforms: *Stillmatic (track)*

- Narrative Magazine (poem of the week): *Lunch Lady Jackie*

- Narrative Magazine: *The Night i Watched my 12 yr Old brother Get Cuffed & Taken From Our home, Tearing, Saying: "i didn't do it!" (Parts 1-4)*

- LittHub: *Survivor's Guilt: A Villanelle*

- The BreakBeat Poets Volume 4 LatiNext Anthology: *Survivor's Guilt: A Villanelle*

- Raising Mothers: *What A Pretty Little Girl*

- Raising Mothers: Lost Seed: *An Abecedarian for Fatherless Daughters*

- Passenger Pigeon Press's "Mojiganga" by Kenny Rivero: *When You Were Red*

# Thank Yous

To my mother: thank you for this life, the sweet songs you sang to me every night, and for sparking my lifelong passion for poetry. To my brothers: thank you for your love and protection. I am the woman I am today because of you. To my entire family: thank you for your support and love; especially my beautiful nieces Kayla Milagro and Katelyn Rocio, my beloved nephew Duany, and my little-big brother Carlos.

To Dr. Mahogany L. Browne, you truly are your sister's keeper. This book would not exist without your heroic love and compassion. Thank you for helping this lifelong dream finally come true. I am eternally grateful. I love you with my whole heart.

To Tongo Eisen-Martin and Black Freighter Press, thank you for believing in this book. But more importantly, thank you for creating a press where writers feel valued and respected.

To Kamilah Aisha Moon, the first to ever edit this manuscript, I hope I've made you proud and that you are resting in blissful purple peace. You are deeply missed. Endless gratitude to my brilliant editors: Jehan Roberson, Ishion Hutchinson, Caroline Rothstein, Lisandra Ramos, and Tali Gumbiner. Without your wise and loving feedback, this book would not be what it is.

To the GOAT and my forever favorite poet, Willie Perdomo, your work carried me throughout my life, and your friendship has sustained me to date. Thank you for existing. Aire.

To my dearest friends who held me during the writing of this book: Taray Stewart, Keisha Whitehair, Sharif Fakhr, Kenny Rivero, Alba Rosario, Denia Burdie, Jennifer Rodriguez, Adalberto Fernandez, Frank Soto, Jive Poetic, Carlos Andreas Gomez, Gilberto Gutierrez, Frank Lopez, Karen Jaime, Jarina De Marco, Irka Mateo, and Substantial, to name a few. With a giant shout-out to Rico Frederick for designing this book. Most importantly, no one has read more of my poems than Reina Yolanda Burdie. I am a better poet because of her. Thank you. You will all forever have my love and gratitude.

To my poetry community at Cave Canem, especially Dante Micheaux, Tracie Morris, Tyehimba Jess, and the unforgettable 2022 Group B Coven. To the most sacred space, The Nuyorican Poets Cafe, for being a home to all poets. To my NYU MFA classmates and faculty for giving me all the tools a poet can handle, especially, Deborah Landau, Meghan O'Rourke, Matt Rohrer, Robin Coste-Lewis, Ishion Hutchinson, Nick Laird, and Catherine Barnett. Special shout-out to John Freeman, your belief in me post-graduation made me believe in me. Thank you.

Most importantly, to my children, being your mother is by far my greatest achievement. You're such dope kids. I just want you to be as proud of me as I am of you. Chase your dreams, they want to be caught.

## Author's Bio

Anacaona Rocio Milagro is a poet born, raised, and living in New York City, Washington Heights. She is the daughter of Oshun but was adopted by Yemaya. Her father is from the Dominican Republic and her mother is from St. Thomas, The U.S. Virgin Islands. Writing poetry since age four and performing throughout her life, she hit the national stage with the Nuyorican Poets Café Slam team in the National Poetry Slam competition. She earned an MFA in Poetry at NYU's Residency program in Paris and an MPH from Columbia University. She earned a BA in Social Anthropology and Journalism/Creative Writing with a minor in Art from Baruch College. However, nothing compares to her education from the prestigious school of hard knocks. Today, she is a Cave Canem Fellow. She has published in Narrative Magazine, The BreakBeat Poets Latinext Anthology, Haper's Bazaar Magazine, The Common, LittHub, Writing The Land Anthology: Currents, No Dear Magazine, and others. Her *Nine Eleven Poem* has been added to the Smithsonian Museum's 9/11 archives. Her debut spoken-word poetic track *Stillmatic* is available on all streaming platforms. Instagram: @poet.anacaona

"There's a ship
The Black Freighter
With a skull on it's masthead
Will be coming in"

— Nina Simone, Pirate Jenny

**Black Freighter Press** publishes revolutionary books. committed to the exploration of liberation, using art to transform consciousness. A platform for Black and Brown writers to honor ancestry and propel radical imagination.